Mike,

Best of Luck!

# Additional Comments

"These techniques have been proven to be effective for me.
The ideas are flexible enough to adapt them
to your personality."
*Christen L. Myers,* Corporate Information Systems Analyst
NORSTAN COMMUNICATIONS

"Degrees and skills are only part of what employers look at
when considering a job candidate. Whether employers
realize it or not, they are really hiring the individual, the
personality. And if they are not they should be, because
fitting into the organization, flexibility, and the ability to
communicate are proven qualities of the best employees.
Technical skills can be taught, people skills can't. How
Hard Are You Knocking? could possibly be the most valuable 'textbook' a college student could use. Read it, study it
seriously like your final grade depends on it, because it
very well may have more effect on you career
than anything else you have studied."
*Janet Palcko,* General manager
NEO ADMINISTRATION COMPANY
President
SALES & MARKETING EXECUTIVES OF AKRON

"A Fantastic book which reveals helpful guidelines to
attaining your first job out of college. This book gives
college graduates clear, simple examples that are often
overlooked costing the interviewee the opportunity to
succeed. The perfect self-help book for the graduating
senior on the market today."
*Michael Platt,* Corporate Recruiter
UNITECH SYSTEMS, INCORPORATED

# How Hard
# Are
# You Knocking?

# How Hard Are You Knocking?

## The College Student's Guide to Opening Corporate Doors

by
Timothy Augustine
with
Rana Curcio

**Oakhill Press**
**Akron • New York**

# How Hard Are You Knocking?

**Library of Congress Cataloging-in-Publication Data**

Augustine, Timothy, 1971 -
  **How Hard Are You Knocking? : the college student's guide to opening corporate doors/** by Timothy J Augustine with Rana Curcio.
    120 pp.
  ISBN 1-886939-08-X (pb) : $12.95
  1. Job hunting. 2. Applications for positions. 3. Resumes (Employment)
  4. Employment interviews. 5. College graduates - Employment. I.
  Curcio, Rana, 1971 -        . II. Title.

HF5382.7.A86        1996
650.14--dc20                                96-15403
                                                 CIP

**0 9 8 7 6 5 4 3 2 1**

First Printing, April 1996

In memory of
Aaron Patrick Aldous
October 22, 1984-June 20, 1987

# Acknowledgments

We would like to take this opportunity to thank the following individuals for contributing to the success of *How Hard Are You Knocking?* Your inspiration and friendship will never be forgotten! We would like to thank Hal Becker, James A. Butler, Chris Carter, Eddy Chiochetti, Calvin Carstensen, Jane Hetzel, Sidney Landskroner, Michael Losneck, Michael Lynch, Steven Marks, Janet Palcko, Lisa Smith, John Stoker, Renate Tilgner, Timothy Viezer, and Karl Ziellenbach. We also thank AM Akron Toastmasters International Club, Beta Pi Chapter of Delta Sigma Pi and Kent State University, the Staff at Kent State University Career Services Center, and the entire team at Unitech Systems, Inc. Most importantly, we would like to thank our family and friends for your continued love and support.

# Contents

# 1

## How Hard Are You Knocking?

Before you read any further, take a piece of paper and write down **everything** you have done in the past 24 hours. This includes eating, sleeping, talking on the phone, going on a date - absolutely everything. When you are finished, continue reading.

This exercise was to see how busy you are. Was there a time in your day when you did absolutely nothing? Probably not! That is the reason this book is perfect for you; I want you to take at least one hour to read through it. The reason? This book will enable **you** to change *your* life! This allocation of time will dramatically change at least one detail in your life which will enable you to get the job you deserve after college.

I began my job search while I was preparing for my last semester in college. The first step was to visit a library and begin the research process. What book should I check out? Which one is best? Which one will I have time to read and actually use? These types of questions are asked by many college students. There are many books published on specific topics. A 300 page resume book, a 250 page book on dressing properly, a 400 page book on interviewing, and many others. All of these books are great, but what college student has the time to read each one? We are busy preparing for graduation as well as, our lives after college.

This book illustrates a brief set of guidelines which every college student *will* have time to read and apply to his or her job search. This book is small enough to fit into your back pocket and to read in about a week's time. I put it together by compiling everything I learned in the job market so that you, the college student, would be able to apply these skills in a timely manner. Recently graduating from college and going through a rigorous job search process, I can empathize with college students of the 90's. I believe this book will help.

This is not rocket science. This is just what I have found to be successful in my endeavors and experiences in the "real" world. Who better to understand what you are going through than a 24 year old college graduate who wanted a great job, and got one. Like you, I did not have the time to read 2000 pages to find it.

This book contains guidelines which can help you during the decision making process. It is designed to give you tools that will help you market your knowledge, personality, and accomplishments. This book incorporates my college experiences, so you can profit from the mistakes which I made. I hope it will allow you to adapt your own past experiences to effectively market yourself effectively.

This is the time to start thinking about the future! *How Hard Are You Knocking?* will instruct you on how to do everything from researching a company to dressing for the interview, to following up afterward. These techniques have helped many college students obtain the jobs they wanted. These techniques have also established effective methods for college students to market themselves. As you read this book, apply your own personal touches. Your experiences will come alive through your ideas and knowledge.

# 2

## In the Beginning...

What is college? College is the time to grow, to experience new things and to take risks. You have the opportunity to be daring and to come out of your shell. It is the chance to build memories, make friends, and maybe meet a significant other. College is also the time to make decisions, and to strive for results. You should establish goals and decide what you want out of life. It is a stepping stone for your success as you develop your own personal strengths and accomplishments.

College is different for everyone. Some people think it is just time to party away from home and do whatever they want. Others take this time to study and to achieve results. To be successful, however, you should seek a balance. Believe me, I had my share of fun in college, but I was also able to accomplished my goals. This is because I learned early in my college career to manage my time and priorities effectively.

College is also the time to meet people and learn from them. You are what you are because of the people you have been in contact with your entire life. Think about it. Your personality, trust, honesty, have been learned from the people who have surrounded you. Every person with whom we come in contact, leaves something behind. When I meet someone whom I think is a good listener, I try to incorporate that quality within my own personality. I try to take that trait and develop good listening skills.

College is the time to begin networking. Your personality could be your resume. Everyone you meet has the potential to be a career contact. During college, you are faced with numerous opportunities to meet a wide variety of people. People you meet in your classes, dorm, or even the bar could be possible job contacts. For instance, one of my friends was offered a job two years after college because of a referral from an old dorm roommate!

You can also meet people through organizations. You can join college organizations as well as community organizations. The key is to get involved and become active with whatever you decide to do. There are many opportunities to join organizations within your field. These organizations can put you in contact with people who have the same goals and ideas as you. Who knows, you may be establishing a friendship with a president of a huge company. For example, my first job out of college was the result of an offer from a company Chief Executive Officer. He was in my Toastmaster's Club, a professional speaking organization.

There are many organizations to join in college. The first step is to gather information. There is usually a department for student activities on campus. Next, decide which organizations sound interesting to you. Then, attend one of their meetings. Even if you are just a little interested, try it. Give yourself a choice of several organizations. Make sure you do not spread your time too thin. It is better to give everything you have to one organization rather than too little time to multiple organizations. It is a good idea to join diverse organizations which will help you develop into a well-rounded person. Join the ones that you feel you can help and which, in turn, will help you. Be yourself and give it your best. You may not see your impact on that club, but the members you have influenced will remember. Organizations will make your college life memorable. Some of the organizations that I joined were *Delta Sigma Pi*, a professional business fraternity, and *Toastmasters International*, a professional speaking organization. The organizations helped me develop my skills and assisted me in reaching my college and career goals. These organizations helped me develop leadership skills, listening skills, and delegation skills. They also allowed me to partake in activities in which I worked in teams on projects and made contributions to the community.

During your networking, try to find a person whom you admire, a person who has been where you want to be and who knows what needs to be done to be successful. Ask this person to become your coach. When I refer to a coach, I am referring to someone who can help in the job search process. This person may also be considered a mentor. He or she should guide you in the right direction and teach you what they know about the field you desire to pursue.

Even the best people need coaches. The million dollar quarterback on a professional football team is out on the field. The team is on the two yard line. The quarterback calls time-out and runs to get advice from the coach. You have already made it down the field during your education and college experience. You are on the two yard line. Now, let someone teach you how to make a touchdown and get the job.

College is what you make it. This is the time to hold on to the memories and the time to really distinguish yourself. It is the time to learn which decisions were right and which were wrong. You are on your own to decide your future, your goals and what you can accomplish. Your personality and interviewing skills are what sells a college student lacking in experience to an employer. College is the time to hone these skills. Join organizations that will help you grow and from which you can learn while having a blast doing it. The key to college success is the ability to balance serious activity with fun.

The reason I keep talking about holding on to the moment is because I miss the parties and the organizations, but I still have all the memories. I loved college and really enjoyed the people I met. There are a lot of memories I would love to bring back to life; there are also a lot of memories that I would love to forget! I know how hard college is, and I also know what college is like in the nineties. Jobs are tough, and it is hard to distinguish yourself from the other million college students around the world. Hopefully, this book will help you profit from my mistakes and also help you know yourself. Be yourself, and you will make the right decisions. Continue to strive for success.

# 3

## The Search has Begun

"Genius is
one percent inspiration
and
ninety-nine percent
perspiration."

-Thomas Edison

The actual job search can be time-consuming and frustrating. However, there are steps you can take to insure you spend your time wisely and efficiently. As you read this section, you will learn how to successfully research various companies which interest you as well as occupations available in your chosen field.

One of the first steps is to define a basic outline in order to structure your search. As a result of my own experiences, I have formulated the following outline and recommend it as a solid course of action.

## Outline

I.    Define your goals  (Where do you want to be in five years?)

II.   Define your objectives  (How are you going to attain your goals?)

III.  Evaluate the steps to reach your objectives/goals

IV.   Research the companies that will help you reach your goals

V.    Resources needed during this process  (Library, Online, etc.)

VI.   Contact each company which matches your stepping stones

VII.  Informational interview  (Interview to gather information)

VIII. Interview

IX.   Getting the job offer

## Defining Goals

This should be a vital part of your career, now and in the future. It allows you to focus your energies on "the big picture." During this step, you should identify the direction in which you would like to pursue your career. For instance, you may wish to start in a large company and simply work your way up the corporate ladder. Or, you may wish to gain experience from an established company and then try out your entrepreneurial skills by starting your own business. On the other hand, you may want to start off at a large company and move, later, to a smaller one. Whatever your goals, it is important to note that the best goals are those that are defined in some way. These goals provide you with direction toward success.

When developing your goals, it is important to understand the rationale behind your search. Are you motivated largely by money, or is leisure time more valuable to you? Do you want a job that has the allure of travel, or one that keeps you in town and close to family and friends? Do you look forward to managing others or working independently? Conducting this kind of self-analysis will enable you to know yourself better and formulate more finite and attainable goals. The following statements are examples of defined goals:

"I want to be a partner in an accounting firm by the age of 35."

"I want to be located in the Cleveland area to raise my family."

In addition, it is important to be realistic when deciding on future goals. Sure, it would be nice to retire by the age of 30, but this is not a realistic goal for the average college graduate. This brings up another fine point. Be sure your goals are flexible. Life is going to change on you too many times to count. The addition of a spouse, children or elderly parents may change your outlook greatly. In addition, once you get into the working world, you may find that your goals and/or values change. For instance, you may be highly motivated by money now, but after your first job, you may realize that you need more time for family and friends. If you are able to adjust your goals to the changes in your life, you can experience great success!

## Defining Objectives

Once you have a grasp of "the big picture," ( how you would like your life/career to turn out), it is important to define the objectives that will allow you to achieve your goals. These objectives may include different types of jobs or different positions within the same firm.

Look at your objectives as the steps of a ladder. You must map out those steps and use them to reach the "big picture." Each job could be a rung on the ladder of your career. As you ascend the ladder, you are growing, adapting your skills, and learning from others.

## Steps to reach your goals

Once you have defined your objectives, the next step is to evaluate how you are going to reach each one. Paper and a pen can help make the process clear. Place one goal at the top of the page. Beneath the goal, place an objective. This objective is a stepping stone toward your goal. Beneath the objective place five ways you plan to attain the objective.

For example:

Goal: To be a partner of an accounting firm by age 35.

Objective: Obtain entry position in an accounting firm.

Career Steps:

1) Research accounting firms in general.

2) Review entry level positions in those firms.

3) Match experience and education with accounting and define what characteristics are needed for the position.

4) Brush up on skills that are lacking, obtain required certifications etc.

5) Find necessary information at the library, in annual reports, through friends and acquaintances, etc.

As you move up the ladder of success, these steps will change. For instance, once you have your entry position, you will want to seek out the next position to further your advancement toward partnership. The reason this is effective is because you visually see your plan or big picture. For every goal and objective, you will have a plan on which you can focus your efforts.

## Research Companies

Next, you need to determine which companies to research. During this step you must also determine geography and type of work. What type of accounting? Where do I want to live? The purpose of this is to decide where you should begin the job search. The more you can focus during this phase, the less time you will waste in the long run. If you begin this job search by aimlessly sending out resumes and working for a company simply because they offered a job, it will take longer to realize that this is not going to help in obtaining your "big picture." Remember, your reputation always stays with you. If you start a job, realize that it is not what you want to do and quit, you will soon have the reputation of someone who is never satisfied and jumps from job to job. A good rule to follow is to plan to stay at a company for at least one year.

To avoid jumping from job to job or being stuck in a job you hate, you should first do as much research as possible to find what you want to do and what will get you there. I promise you that with a little work now in researching a company, your entire life will turn out better.

Be sure to investigate both large and small companies. Students tend to focus on large corporations as employers when in actuality, small companies have dominated in growth and are hiring twice as fast. According to Dun & Bradstreet's annual *Dun's 5000 Employment Outlook Survey*, firms with fewer than 100 employees were expected to account for almost two-thirds of employment growth in 1995.

The next step is actually doing the research. Where to get the materials? You should first go to the library or career center of your college or university. Start here to find information about the fields you have prepared for and ones that interest you. Your career placement center will probably have some sort of career aptitude or compatibility evaluation you can take. This may help you identify what field interests you and the various positions or titles you can look forward to holding. You should also be able to find information regarding what industries are hiring in the short-term and the outlook for various occupations. In addition, you should discover information regarding salaries and expected working conditions. Furthermore, your library may have CD-ROM and other search devices available. Here, you should be able to locate annual reports and public company financial records. These will help give you an idea of what the company does and how successful it has been. In addition, you may want to find out when the company's fiscal year ends. Most company's have tight budgets at the end of a fiscal year, but have an influx of budgetary monies in the early part of a fiscal year. Therefore, it is best to plan your job search for the early part of a company's fiscal year. Be sure to research each company extensively. Try to narrow the list of potential prospects. There is usually a business librarian or career counselor who can assist (See the Careers Online Chapter for further research advice).

Another research method is networking. Talk to professors, parents, brothers, sisters, roommates, or anyone who might be able to give you a tip about a company, a job, or some connection associated with the company. As you gather networking names, create a card catalog using index cards with the person's name, phone number, occupation and any other important information you may need to use later and especially the person who gave you the contact name! Be sure to save this card catalog. You may contact one of these names years later and find out they may be in a position to hire you. You will be surprised, people hire people they know and like. Use your network and research by word of mouth.

You can also research and network by attending functions where professionals in your field will be in attendance and/or giving a presentation. This is a good opportunity to establish a contact in an organization, and to learn more about the company, what it does, and its prospects for the future. Try to meet the speaker personally if possible. For instance, if a representative of a company is giving a speech on campus one night, try to go up to the speaker afterwards and discuss the speech, the company, or common interests. Be sure to introduce yourself and get their business card if you can. This is networking!

Once this research is complete, you then narrow the prospects. Place the companies into categories, such as large companies, small, growing, stable, or whatever will help you break them down.

Once you have completed your research and believe you have narrowed the search to 15 good companies, contact all 15. This is the step where you will schedule informational interviews. Contact each company and explain to them what you are doing.

" My name is _____ and I am doing research on accounting firms with whom I would like to work. Could you please guide me in the direction of the person with whom I should speak regarding employment?"

Once you have scheduled an informational interview follow the steps in the Informational Interview Chapter in this book.

## Conclusion

In summary, define your specific goals and objectives. This is your stepping stone toward success. Focus on the future and what you need to do to achieve success. The future is entirely what you make of it. You can do what ever you want. Make sure you have the steps mapped out and sustain a positive attitude along the way. Good Luck.

# 4

# The Informational Interview

" A single conversation
across the table
with a wise man
is worth
a month's study
of books."

-Chinese Proverb

We now move to the informational interview. An informational interview is a technique that a prospective employee can use to identify the companies which best fit his or her goals and ambitions. The informational interview is a series of steps which are to be performed by the prospective employee. They are simply guidelines which, when practiced, can illustrate to the company the dedication and responsibility the student possesses. This step should be done prior to scheduling an actual job interviews. It is a part of the search which will lead you to the perfect company. You are simply going to interview in order to obtain more in-depth information about a company. This should *not* be a scam to get your foot in the door. It is simply a technique which provides you with experience in talking to employers and understanding what they look for in college students. It will also help you to get a feel for the interview process. In addition, it allows you to identify the companies which best fit your career goals and objectives.

The following steps illustrate how to plan, organize and conduct just such an interview. The information is written in outline form, making each step easier to follow.

I.    An informational interview begins with a phone call to the prospective company(ies) which you have researched.

A. The first person you contact will likely be the receptionist. He or she should be your first friend in the company.

Note:

I have found through my research that the secretary or receptionist plays a large role in the hiring process. They are often asked questions regarding your phone etiquette. Often they are asked to give their general opinion of the applicants they speak with on the telephone and in person. Therefore, begin selling your skills to this person while gaining valuable information about the company. Make sure you learn his/her name.

1. Your main objective is to build rapport.

2. You should ask them for help. Asking questions will allow you to gather information as well as allow the receptionist to feel that he or she is important and helpful to you.

B. The second person you might talk to is the human resources manager.

1. The human resources manager is the person on whom the informational interview is focused and the person who should be able to answer most of the questions you might have about the company.

a. You should first ask them if they have a moment to talk. Respect their time!

b. You should then reveal your interests in the company and your purpose for the phone call.

"Hello, my name is_____ . Do you have a moment to talk? I am preparing to graduate from Florida State University in Marketing and beginning my job search process. I have done some research on ABC Corp. and am interested in learning more about your

company. I am conducting information interviews on
the companies in which I am interested and would be
honored if I could schedule a fifteen minute appointment with you to ask  five questions about ABC Corp.
Once my research is complete I will be better prepared
for the actual interview process with companies with
which I would like to work."

    c. The next step is to set up  a 15
       minute appointment to ask ques-
       tions about the company.

      (1.) The key to  this interview is to
          build  a business friendship.

      (2.) You should also try to build
          rapport with the interviewer.

   2. You can also use this approach with
     the receptionist.

II.  The second phase to the informational in-
    terview is preparation. Pay attention to
    small details. These will distinguish you
    from other prospective employees.  After
    you contact each company and schedule an
    appointment, prepare a list of questions to
    ask.  Every question should be written prior
    to the informational interview to illustrate
    your professionalism.

    A. The preparation before the interview
       should be thorough and precise.

      1. Have some basic knowledge about the
        company and its business.  Review
        your research and decide what infor-
        mation you are lacking.  Imagine that

you are going to be employed by this company.

2. You should have five to ten detailed questions written out prior to the interview that will give you the best possible facts from which you will draw your final job decision.

Here are a few examples of questions you could ask the person with whom you meet.

-What do you know now about this industry that you didn't know before you entered it?

-Would you have done anything differently?

-What types of characteristics are important for success in this field?

-What advice would you give to a graduating senior?

-Does this field/position require any special education /certifications?

3. Plan what you will wear. Your appearance for the informational interview is very important. (Refer to the "Dressing The Part" chapter for clothing tips.)

4. The next step of preparation is your attitude.

a. You should always give positive feedback to yourself.

(1.) I am a good person.

(2.) I will make a new friend today.

(3.) I am perfect for this company.

III. Everything you have done up to this point has been done in preparation for the actual interview. The next phase to the process is the actual informational interview.

A. The key to a successful interview is selling yourself and getting the information you desire. This point applies to the informational interview and the actual job interview.

1. During the interview, be yourself and smile.

a. Remember, people are largely judged on appearance.

2. You should be personable. Ask questions.

a. Make sure you ask specific questions.

b. Make sure those questions are answered to your understanding.

3. If someone comes into the interview, stand, wait for an introduction, then shake hands.

B. Remember that the interviewer is giving you his/her time and that *you* requested *his/her* help. Be honest with the interviewer. He or she may turn out to be your best friend in the business.

1. **Do not** take a resume with you. This may look like your informational interview is really a job interview and way to get your "foot in the door."

    2. Make sure you stick to your 15 minute appointment. Be punctual! Arriving 5 minutes before the scheduled appointment is sufficient.

  C. The key to an informational interview is to gather needed intelligence and to build friendships that will help you find the best job possible.

IV. The final phase to an informational interview is follow-up after the interview.

  A. This procedure will also distinguish you from other prospective employees.

    1. The same day, no later than the day after the interview, send a hand-written thank-you letter to both the interviewer and the receptionist.

  B. Always remember the people that you meet and call them once a month to stay in contact. Add their names to your list of contacts for networking

    1. Remember to **never burn your bridges** and never do anything that will affect your reputation with that company.

    2. The key to success is to network through your friendships.

In summary, an informational interview is a technique that a prospective employee can use to identify the companies which best fit his or her goals and ambitions. The informational interview is a series of steps

which are to be performed by the prospective employee. They are simple guidelines which, when practiced, can illustrate to the company your dedication
and responsibility. In addition, these interviews can
aid college students in gathering information prior to
graduation and the aggressive job search.

All humans have the potential to find their
dreams. All you have to do is find the resources to make
them reality.

# 5

## Your Ticket To Success

"The closest to
perfection
a  person ever comes
is when
he fills out
a job application form."

-Stanley J. Randall

Your "ticket to success" is your professional resume. It will become a snapshot of your experiences, education and activities. Your "ticket to success," your resume, will be your "ticket" into the world of employment. It will most likely become the first contact an employer has with you. How well it is constructed, will be directly related to whether you are invited for an interview. This chapter will illustrate a set of guidelines which will lead to a successful resume.

You should design the resume on a high quality typewriter or word processor. This gives the impression that you are professional and ready for the business world. In addition, you show that you are serious about obtaining a job and advancing your career. Further, using various fonts allows you to design a resume that is attractive and pleasing to the eye. Often, typewriters and resume software programs are available to students through the university. However, if you cannot type your own resume, there are professional resume services available at various prices. Check with your career center/placement office or the local phone book for a list of resume service providers. Although there is a cost involved when using a professional, you can usually be assured of a top quality job.

Whether typing your own resume or subscribing to a service, be sure to have your resume printed on top quality paper. This resume paper is a thicker, textured paper usually made of at least some cotton and conveys a high quality image. It can be found in copy centers and should be available in your campus bookstore. Lighter colors are best as they are easier to read.

It is most important that your resume be neat and error-free. An error-free resume illustrates attention to detail and pride in your work. Remember, competition for most positions is very strong and the slightest error could cost you the opportunity to prove yourself worthy. Keep the font size between 10 point and 14 point. Smaller than this is difficult to read and larger than this indicates to the employer that you are just trying to fill up space. Two people should edit your resume for errors and clarity of wording. Don't forget about members of the placement office or faculty members; they make great critics!

There are many steps to a professional resume. You will want to choose the ideas which best fit your personality and can get you the job you seek. We will begin with the identification section of a resume. At the very top, you will want to insert your complete name in large bold letters, preferably capital letters. The next step is to insert your complete address. **Do not abbreviate** anything especially street, west, or other commonly abbreviated words. If you wish to identify both a college and permanent address, place them on opposite sides of the paper. I recommend only your current address. This illustrates independence. Whichever you choose, make sure the resume has the addresses at which you can be contacted. Since your goal is to obtain an interview with the firm, they must be able to reach you. Below your address, place your city, state, and zip code. Below this, place your telephone number(s), both day time and evening, including your area code. You may also include an E-mail address if you have one.

Figure A-1

# Timothy J. Augustine

**Campus Address**          **Permanent Address**
430 Lake Hall               2434 East White Street
Miami, Florida 44444        Miami, Florida 44444
(416) 672- 0000             (416) 929-1111

If you have only one address:

## Timothy J. Augustine
2434 East White Street
Miami, Florida 44444
(416) 929-1111

These examples can vary, but are presented here as guidelines that you could follow. Remember that attention to detail could be the deciding factor. Don't let sloppiness or lack of attention to detail contribute to the success of your competitor!

The next step is your career objective. An objective describes your goals to the employer. It should be short and to the point, yet fully illustrate your desire and your professionalism. Remember that an employer has many resumes to review, and sometimes all they look at is your objective.

By asking many professionals during my research, I found that most companies receive about 1000 resumes for a given position. The slightest error, or a poorly written general objective statement could place your resume in the circular file (Trash). Therefore, you need to make your objective statement eye-catching and to the point. It is important to note that employers like to see objective statements that illustrate what you want to do for the company, not what you want the company to do for you. The objective reveals what it is you want to do and the rest of the resume develops the reasons why you are qualified to do it.

You may also use a summary in place of an objective statement. This is often used when the applicant has significant work experience. A summary uses 3-5 strong sentences which highlight your accomplishments and link them to your career goals. You can highlight leadership skills, expertise or personal strengths. Use either an objective or a summary, never both. Figure A-2 illustrates examples of objective and summary statements.

Figure A-2

## OBJECTIVE EXAMPLES

**OBJECTIVE**
To obtain a position in medical supply sales which will give me the opportunity to utilize my communication skills and contribute to the success of the firm.

**OBJECTIVE** Obtain an entry level position in accounting with a financial firm.

**OBJECTIVE**
Obtain a challenging position that requires creativity and communication skills in the field of marketing.

# SUMMARY EXAMPLES

**SUMMARY**
  Bachelors degree in marketing from a four year institution. Excellent communication skills. Speak Italian and Japanese. Experienced in all aspects of marketing research.

**SUMMARY**
  A bachelors degree in Financial Management. Successfully completed an internship with ABC Corporation in Cleveland, Ohio. Developed communication skills through Toastmasters International.

**SUMMARY**
Successfully completed an internship with Main Street Muffins, Akron, Ohio. Excellent communication skills. Experience with Macintosh and IBM personal computers. Traveled and attended schools in Europe and Italy

  These are just a set of guidelines. There are many other ideas that can also be very effective. Bounce ideas off other people during the editing process and create the best resume which reflects your talents and strengths.
  The next step is your education. During this step there are two parts to follow. First, you must list your college education, and second, your high school. The high school education can be left out to save room for your other accomplishments. The high school section is really only needed if applicable in some way. It is assumed that you graduated high school. However, if you do include your high school information, you'll want to list your high school name, followed by the

month and year of graduation. Include this location: class rank, GPA, class honors, and any other significant accomplishments.

First, describe your college education. List your most recent degree first, followed by the month and year of graduation. In this section, you want to list your college, and its location. Illustrate your major(s)/ minors and your GPA if it is greater than 3.0. If your GPA is lower than 3.0 you may not want to put it in writing. If it is not in writing, it may not be remembered by the interviewer. If you paid for most of your education, you want to illustrate this such as, "Financed 100% of Education." This reveals to the interviewer that you are a hard worker who strives for success. The final guideline to this section is your significant course work. List the classes you have taken that are pertinent to your major. However, try not to list more than four courses.

Remember, these are only guidelines to follow. You may decide to give attention to a just a few of these ideas and save space.

Figure A-3

## EDUCATION EXAMPLES

**EDUCATION**
Bachelor of Business Administration, May 1994
Ohio State University, Columbus, Ohio
Major: Accounting
GPA: 3.5

Diploma, May 1990
Mansfield High School, Mansfield, Ohio

**EDUCATION**
Columbia University, New York, NY
Bachelor of Business Administration, December 1996
Major: Marketing, GPA: 4.0

**EDUCATION**
Master of Business Administration, May 1996
Wharton School of Business, Philadelphia, PA
Concentration: Finance
GPA: 3.2

Bachelor of Business Administration
Duke University
Major: Finance  GPA: 4.0

The next section is work experiences. It can have a myriad of titles such as Related Work Experience, Business Experience, Professional Experience, Internship, or Other Experience. Begin with the most recent experience. The first step is usually to list the title of the position you held. This is often done if your position is with a smaller firm with which others may not be familiar. On the other hand, you may wish to start the first line with the name of the company. This is often done when the firm is a large well-known corporation. Either is appropriate, however, each listing must be in the same form. In other words, if you list your position first in the most recent job listing, you must follow the same format for the other listings. If you start with the position title first, do likewise with all other entries. The next step, is to reference the company or organization and the location, including city and state. Also, insert the dates of employment, either in the margin or within the description.

The final step is to describe your experience and responsibilities. Try to use phrases rather than entire sentences and eliminate all personal pronouns such as *I, me,* and *my.* In this step you will want to use past tense action words such as achieved, coordinated, designed, etc. Describe how well you did the job and explain your accomplishments during the experience. See figure A-4.

Another suggestion is to use nouns specifically related to your field. These are often buzz words for which employers often look. For instance, include specific products, services, or programs with which you are familiar. One example would be, "Conducted order entry of stocks, bonds and mutual funds." Upon scanning this resume, the employer immediately notices that you are familiar with specific products that are used in that industry.

This is a very important section, and one that you should spend some time on. Be creative in your descriptions. Take the everyday tasks and turn them into traits useful to the employer. For instance, avoid general job descriptions such as *clerical work, filing,* or *answering phones.* Instead, depict these tasks as "office management, organization and retrieval of information, and customer service operations." Take each task that you performed and illustrate how the experience has prepared you for other jobs. Be sure to use examples of experiences that relate to the job you are *trying* to obtain. Too often, students just list every job they have had and what they did just to have it written on the resume. Instead, it is important to understand the skills required for the position you are applying for, and emphasize those traits! For instance, if you worked for four years as a waitress/waiter but had a one semester internship in the field of your choice, elaborate on the description of the internship and be brief with the server job description. This will emphasize the experience that is directly related to your career goals and downplay jobs you have taken just for the money. You can find examples in Figure A-4.

The following is a list of action words you may want to use.

Accomplished
Achieved
Acquired
Administered
Advised
Appointed
Assessed
Assisted
Assured
Brought
Budgeted
Chaired
Collaborated
Communicated
Composed
Controlled
Coordinated
Delegated
Demonstrated
Developed
Educated
Encouraged
Established
Evaluated
Expedited

Formulated
Fostered
Implemented
Initiated
Integrated
Motivated
Maintained
Negotiated
Organized
Persuaded
Produced
Programmed
Recommended
Researched
Reviewed
Selected
Started
Strengthened
Supervised
Targeted
Transformed
Tutored
Unearthed
Worked

Figure A-4

## WORK EXPERIENCE EXAMPLES

### RELATED EXPERIENCE

1990- 1994   **Sales Associate**, Green Lumber Company, Denver, CO.
Established new accounts, ordered merchandise, responsible for accounts payable and payroll

### WORK EXPERIENCE

**Ski Instructor**, Snow Trails, Pittsburgh, PA
* Organized ski trips for area youth
* Educated skiers on winter safety
* Instructed groups of 50 Skiers
* Developed and presented teamwork ski programs

### OTHER WORK EXPERIENCE

Computer Director, Main Street Muffins, Akron, Ohio

Developed training classes on computer methods, analyzed omputer programs and updated existing mainframe.

1992- present.

The work experience section of a resume reveals to the employer what you can do, as well as what you have accomplished. Make each point stand out in order to reveal your hard work and to also illustrate your devotion to past jobs. Consistency is the important key in this section of resume writing. If you use bold face type for your position in one instance, use it for your position every time. Notice the dates in the examples. They can either be in months or years. I prefer years because this might visually give you a full year more work experience. During the interview you will discuss the exact timing of past jobs, but this might get you past the front door or past the "gate keeper" reviewing the resumes. I am not suggesting that you lie to the employer. I am only suggesting that if you quit a job on February 1, 1995 and you worked for the company since November 1, 1993 you can put (1993-1995), even though the actual time has been 15 months. Again, these are only examples. You are the best at distinguishing yourself and making your accomplishments stand out, so go with what you feel. Remember to be honest, professional, creative, and most importantly: **pay attention to detail!**

The next step is to illustrate leadership experience and extra-curricular activities. This shows energy, initiative and interpersonal skills. In this section you will also want to use past tense action words. Your goal is to show how well you performed during these experiences. First, list the position(s) held and state the name of the organization. You will also want to include the location of the organization and indicate the time span of the position. Figure A-5 gives leadership examples.

Figure A-5

## LEADERSHIP EXAMPLES

<u>Leadership skills</u>

**President**, ABC Leadership Board, ABC University

Planned monthly meetings and secured professional speakers.

Followed Robert's Rules of Order, functioned as a liaison between student body and faculty. (1993-1994).

**Vice-President**, Ski Club, Chicago, IL (1994-1995).

Assisted the president with management of this 80 member club.

Planned trips to Denver and instructed new members on different techniques of skiing.


**President** Delta Sigma Pi, Professional Business Fraternity.

Miami University (1994-1995).

Formulated the structure for the 80 member Miami Chapter and all of its activities.


After leadership roles, follow the honors and activities section. In this section you will want to list the activities in which you are active and/or honors received in college. Also, list your high school activities and/or honors only if they are significant or applicable and only if high school education was included in your Educational section. Examples of these are found in Figure A- 6.

Figure A- 6

## HONORS AND ACTIVITY EXAMPLES

**HONORS/ACTIVITIES:**

<u>COLLEGE</u>                    <u>HIGH SCHOOL</u>

Dean's list, six semesters        Valedictorian

National Dean's list 1990         Honor roll

Delta Sigma Pi Golden Key Award

Kent Interhall Council

### Honors

  *Collegian of the Year 1994

  *Dean's list eight semesters

  *Delegate of Kent State, Beta Pi Chapter, Delta Sigma Pi

Next step is your hobbies and interests. This section shows the employer you are a well rounded individual. You may want to outline your travel experience, hobbies, and special interests. This section is optional and is often used only if space is available. Depending on the job and the company, you may want to consider not placing this section on your resume. Examples can be found in Figure A-7

Figure A- 7

## HOBBIES/INTERESTS EXAMPLES

### INTERESTS

Golfing, hunting, fishing, and reading

### PERSONAL INTERESTS

Camping, spectator sports, golf, boating, fishing

The purpose of illustrating your hobbies is to establish common ground with the employer and illustrate how well rounded you are. Do not try to make up hobbies because the interviewer may ask you about the hobbies and you will have no clue what to say. Remember to always be honest. Your reputation stays with you.

The final section is the reference section. It usually states that character references can be provided if necessary. This is now considered an optional section. It is often assumed that references will be available upon request. Therefore, you may choose to omit this section if you wish to conserve space. On the other hand, you may desire to include the actual list of references with your resume. In this case, you would simply list each references name, title, company, address and phone on a second page of your resume. If you do include references, have three to four names. Examples of these reference sections are in Figure A-8.

Figure A- 8

## REFERENCE EXAMPLES

**References:**  Available upon request.

**References:**
    Joe Smith
    Vice President of Manufacturing
    Motorola
    123 Park Way
    Chicago, IL 99999
    (123)456-7890

You should always have your references with you during your interview. The interviewer may request them. Make sure they are neat originals like your resume. You should take letters of reference to the interview in case they are requested.

## Cover Letter

When mailing your resume, you will need to enclose a cover letter. This is a simple letter designed to give an overview of your objectives and qualifications. It should be addressed to a specific person. Find out the name of the human resources director rather than addressing the letter to "dear sir or madam." The letter should be about three to four paragraphs long and convey your interest in a position with the prospective firm.

Following are examples of resumes and cover letters which will apply the guidelines mentioned in this chapter. Analyze each of them. Take different ideas from them and build *your own* perfect resume and cover letter which represents you best.

# JANE DOE
1000 Oak Lane
Columbus, Ohio 44240
(555) 777-1000

**Objective:**    To obtain a human resources position with an organization which affords me the opportunity to contribute through my knowledge and experience.

**Education:**    Ohio State University
Bachelor of Business Administration
Major: Human Resource Management (3.0 GPA)
May 1995

**Experience:**    *Internship*, - Columbus Direct , Columbus, Ohio
Assisted in customer accounts and established new clients through direct mailings and cold calls.

*Server /Trainer*, Mario's, Cuyahoga Falls, Ohio.
Established training programs for new employees. Maintained daily cash flows of $500.00. Responsible for enthusiastic quality service.

*Data Entry Specialist*, King Office Products, New Philadelphia, Ohio
Responsible for inventory control and merchandise levels for daily operation. Conducted monthly ordering of office supplies.

*Customer Service Representative*, Andy's Shoes, New Philadelphia,Ohio.
Developed promotional programs for in-house sales displays. Assisted customers with purchases while maintaining product knowledge.

**Professional Organizations:**    **Society for Human Resource Management**
Recognition Director
Formulated recognition programs for students professional development in other organizations during their college career.
Director of Administration
Devised administrative data documenting student activities.
External Affairs Chair
Maintained correspondence with alumni and other chapters. Acted as a liaison between the local SHRM chapter and the OSU College of Business.

**New Student Orientation Instructor**

**College of Business Administration Student Ambassador**

**Honors/Awards:**    Golden Rose Society Award
Ohio State University Outstanding Service Award
Ohio State University Orientation Micro Teacher Award
Ohio State University Homecoming Court Nominee
Deans List Award

**References:**    Available upon request

# ROBERT JONES
100 West Main Street ◆ Beverly Hills, California 90210
E-mail: RJONES@usc.edu

## OBJECTIVE:
To obtain a position within the field of finance with a firm in which I can contribute and grow.

## EDUCATION:
| | |
|---|---|
| Bachelor of Business Administration | West Beverly High School |
| University of Southern California- August 1996 | Diploma - May 1992 |
| GPA: 3.73 | Beverly Hills, California |
| Major: Finance | |

## BUSINESS EXPERIENCE:
**The Prudential California Realty** - Beverly Hills, California
Real Estate Assistant   1994 to present
   ◆ Involved in transactions totaling over $1 million
   ◆ Coordinated closings with loan officers and processors as well as escrow agents
   ◆ Designed marketing plans and financial budgets for client listings.

**Merrill Lynch** -Los Angeles, California
Intern  1993 - 1994
   ◆ Conducted trade order entry of stocks, bonds, and mutual funds via wire system
   ◆ Handled receipt and disbursement of funds and securities
   ◆ Opened and updated estate, trust, and custodial accounts
   ◆ Assisted in promoting and implementing marketing strategy for financial planning
   ◆ Recorded daily transactions in client ledgers
   ◆ Conducted data searches to obtain information about securities

## LEADERSHIP:
**Sr. Vice President** - Delta Sigma Pi,  Professional Business Fraternity, USC (1994)
-Devised recruitment plan to elicit members and reconstructed new officer training process

**Public Relations Chair**- Accounting Association,  USC (1993)
-Programmed speakers and presentations for chapter meetings

## HONORS:
| | |
|---|---|
| 100% Tuition | Golden Key National Honor Society |
| All University Leadership Award | President's List and Dean's List |
| Beta Gamma Sigma | Alpha  Lambda Delta Honorary |

## SKILLS:
IBM and Macintosh: spreadsheet, word processing and presentation software
Financial software programs
Dale Carnegie Course Training in Human relations

## ACTIVITIES:
Financial Management Association
Community Service: Adopt-a-Highway, Toe-to-Tow Marathon, food and clothing drives
USC Rollerblade Club

## Bill Smith

222 West Broad Street
Orlando, Florida 12345
Phone: (313) 444-5555

**SUMMARY:** A Bachelors degree in Marketing. Fluent in French and Italian. Studied abroad in Florence, Italy. Excellent communication Skills.

**EDUCATION:**

**Florida State University**
Bachelor of Business Administration
Major: Marketing 4.0,       December 1994

**1993**     **Dale Carnegie Training Course**
Received the scholarship by competing against eighty college students for this professional leadership presentation award. Graduated: August 1993 from twelve week course

**1993-present   Toastmasters International**
Professional presentation organization. Earned Competent Toastmaster in less than 1 1/2 years. The youngest member among 45 professionals
Public Relations Director
Developed and implemented club activities to culture team building skills and to represent the professionalism to the community

**EXPERIENCE:**

**1995-present** *Sales Associate,* Steelhead, Inc. Orlando, Florida
Responsible for prospecting, lead generation. Identified and pursued qualified prospects.
Professionally, ethically, and accurately sold Steelhead products and services
Demonstrated customer-focused problem solving skills

**1994-present** *Total Quality Management Instructor,* Total Management Solutions, Orlando, Florida
Assisted in the implementation of Total Quality Management to various companies and industries. Assisted in the development of the TQM manual used by the Clients

**1993-1994** *Regional Sales Associate,* MainFocus Printing, Orlando, Florida
Responsible for Akron/Canton region for special accounts. Established 55% new accounts in less than one year. Serviced 145 internal and external accounts

**1988-1992** *Sales Consultant,* ACE Lumber Company, Orlando, Florida
Established customer relations for professional outside sales of building supplies. Developed blueprints for buildings and decks to internal and external accounts

Bill Smith                                          Page 2

**PROFESSIONAL**
**ORGANIZATIONS:**
**1993-1995    American Marketing Society**
President
Formulated the structure of the 80 member organiza-
tion and its activities
Executive board officer of Fundraising
Coordinated all monetary activities incorporated into
the organization to allow self sufficient funding of all
activities

**1993-1994    Student Leadership Development Board,** Elected Student representative
Publicity Director
Devised publicity efforts and cultivated marketing con-
cepts to represent the organization

**1992-1993    Business Administration Presidents' Roundtable**
Chaired the elected position and represented students
of the college of Business

**COMMUNITY**
**INVOLVEMENT**
**1994-present  Communication Society**
Established professional presentation workshops, pub-
licized student development programs

**1993-present  Johnstown Baseball Coach**
Coached boys 12-14 year old team. Served as a role
model and teacher. Established team building skills,
communication skills, and sportsmanship skills

**VALUED**
**ATTRIBUTES:**

| | |
|---|---|
| **Customer -Focused** | **Self Disciplined** |
| **Excellent Communication Skills** | **Honesty** |
| **Self Motivated** | **Genuine** |
| **Ethical** | **Team Player** |
| **Goal Oriented** | **Leadership** |
| **Excellent Organizational Skills** | |
| **Ability and Willingness to Learn** | |

**HONORS**
**AWARDS:**

Collegian of the Year- Florida State University
Student Leader of the Year- Florida State University
Leadership Excellence Award-Florida State University
Student Leader of the Month, 6 months- Florida State University
Education leadership award- American Marketing Association
Presidents Award- Business Administration Roundtable
Golden Board Education Award- Communication Society
Golden Rose Society- Florida State University
Table Topic Award- Toastmaster International

## Jane Doe

555 East Third Street
Jacksonville, Florida 55555
(888) 567-0000

April 17, 1995

Mr. John Smith
Director
Florida State Social Services
600 Water Street
Jacksonville, Florida   55555

Dear Mr. Lloyd:

In August 1995, I will receive my Bachelor of Arts degree from Florida State University, pending the completion of my foreign language requirement, and I am interested in obtaining a position with your agency.

As you will see from the enclosed resume, I majored in Psychology and Criminal Justice, and achieved a 3.0 and 3.2 G.P.A. respectively. For the past one and a half years, I have been employed as a case manager at the Florida Temporary Homeless Shelter, and volunteered at the same agency for six months prior to my present employment. This experience has afforded me the opportunity to learn the functions of a homeless shelter, and allowed me to participate in decisions regarding updating shelter policies and documentation procedures.

Realizing that this summary, as well as my resume, can not adequately communicate my qualifications in depth, I would appreciate the opportunity to discuss withyou in person how I might become an asset to your agency.

Sincerely,


Jane Doe

Enclosure

## Julie Smith
1144 West Barley Road ◆ St. Louis, Missouri 77001
(555)111-2222


September 1, 1996

Ms. Margaret Evans
Regional Director of Human Resources
ABC Corporation
Naperville, Illinois  60540

Dear Ms. Evans:

I am writing in reference to the advertised employment opportunity in the marketing department at ABC.  I will finish my coursework towards a Bachelors of Business Administration and will receive my degree in December of this year.  Please accept my resume and letter for your review.

My business experience and educational endeavors have prepared me for a career in the field of marketing.  I have worked as a sales representative for several years which has captured my interests.  In addition, I have had success in my course work and shall be graduating with honors.

The enclosed resume highlights several other achievements, experiences, and awards.  I have also had extensive involvement in work, classes, and various organizations in which I had opportunities to perform individually and as part of a team.  Further, I have strengthened my skills in human relations, communications, and leadership through my co-curricular activities.

I would welcome an opportunity to meet with you to discuss my qualifications.  Please contact me at (222)333-4444.  I may also be contacted via the Internet at jsmith@aol.com.

Sincerely,


Julie Smith

Enclosure

## James Jackson

123 Wilson Drive
Phoenix, Arizona 00446
(818)222-9999

September 5, 1996

Mr. Edward Smiles
XYZ Corporation
Rochester, New York 80011

Dear Mr. Smiles:

Wouldn't you agree that in today's telecommunications industry, fresh ideas and forward thinking individuals are the key to sustaining a competitive advantage?

While attending the University of Colorado, I gained hands-on training of the latest technological advancements in the telecommunications field. In addition, as President of the American Marketing Association at UC, I designed new marketing efforts which effectively increased membership over 30% in just one year. Further, as a Student Senator, I was a part of crafting vision and mission statements for the student body.

I will be receiving Bachelors degree in Marketing and Communications in December of this year and am currently searching for employment opportunities. Enclosed is my resume and list of references. I believe I would make an immediate and positive contribution to your firm. In addition, relocation to the New York area would not present problem.

I would welcome the opportunity to discuss the possibility of employment with your firm. Please contact me at (818)222-9999.

Sincerely,

James Jackson

Enclosure

# 6

## Career Info Online

There are a multitude of resources available to aid in your job search, and more are being introduced each day. One important channel available to most college students, is the Internet. This vast resource is expanding every day. More importantly, you don't even need to be a computer "hacker" to reap the benefits these days.

Almost all colleges and universities are now online in one form or another. This is a tremendous benefit to students, and not only for finding a job. If your college is not online, chances are it soon will be. The first step for the job seeker is to get an account through the university in order to log on to the Internet. This should be free of charge for students. You will need to check with the appropriate department in your college in order to obtain the account if necessary. (One place to start might even be with a tutor in the computer lab.) If your university does not have access to the Internet, or you are no longer a student, there are many other service providers who can assist you. America Online, Prodigy, Netcom, and CompuServ, are just a few. The software for these services can be purchased for a small cost at most computer retailers. Many of these companies offer free introduction packets so you can try their service before actually purchasing the product or subscribing to the service.

One of the first things you will want to do is set up an E-mail address. This will be specific according to the particular provider. For example, E-mail on America Online is username@aol.com. Most universities will end with .edu such as with TimA@bsa1.kent.edu. Electronic mail is important for several reasons. First of all, you will be providing a way for potential employers to contact you via the Internet. In addition, even if you know nothing about computers and technology, you will appear to be up to date with the latest technological trends. As previously mentioned, you may want to include your E-mail address on resumes that you send to prospective employers.

Once you have an account and are set up with E-mail, it is time to explore the Internet and World Wide Web. The following instructions may be geared to America Online, however, most Internet access is user friendly and can be easily navigated with a bit of practice. If you are using a provider through your university and are not familiar with the Internet, you may want to speak with the computer lab assistant. In addition, it is often possible to hire a tutor who can show you how to "surf the 'net."

One of the quickest ways to get started with your search may be to use one of the search vehicles available through most providers. These include programs such a gopher, Web Crawler, and others. These programs allow you search the web for any variety of topics. You simply type in the words you wish to search for and the program brings up lists of locations where these words are found. For instance, you could select Web Crawler and ask it to search for "jobs." This will return tens of thousands of possible locations which contain the word "jobs" somewhere in their text. These are good starting places to explore what the 'net has to offer for employment.

In addition, many of the Internet providers have set up pre-designed destinations which offer the most sought after information. Occupational profiles are just one aid available online. These are detailed descriptions of occupations. It is important to take a look at several possible positions in your chosen field to see what each job entails. On America Online, this category is under "reference desk" of the main menu. The subheading is "occupational profiles." Most providers carry this type of reference guide, although it may be under a slightly different title. The user simply enters the word or words which are related to his/her field. For instance, your major might be a great place to start (i.e. finance, biology, education, etc.). Other words to search may be specific jobs you are interested in such as financial analyst, genetic engineer, or teacher. The appropriate information will be retrieved and displayed on the screen. It then becomes a matter of selecting which job title looks interesting and exploring it further. Information contained in this area should include work descriptions, work conditions, places of employment, education and training requirements, salary expectations, job demand outlook/forecasts, other related occupations, required personal traits, lifestyle implications and more. In fact, America Online even provides information on what actions to take to find out more about the profession. This occupational profile is a beneficial source for finding information before the interview. Furthermore, with the occupational profile, you can eliminate any professions which do not fit with your goals or tastes. Although it is possible that your provider does not have this exact program, it will probably have similar programs which illustrate what certain jobs entail.

The provider will most likely have some sort of career or employment information program. On America Online, this is titled the "Career Center." This area is full of free information and job searches. Often, there are articles on various employment-related subjects, as well as explanations and help services.

One of the first items in America Online is the "Talent Bank." This is a list of resumes of job seekers. Employers can search this database and screen it as they would any pool of applicants. In this section, you may enter your resume information and be included in the talent bank. This information can later be updated or deleted from the file. For an additional fee, you can have your resume entered into the worldwide resume/talent bank. At last check, this was $40 and kept you resume online for one year. This will allow 24 hour access to your resume by over 30 million online users in the US and worldwide. Step by step instructions are given which illustrate how to go about putting your resume in the Talent Bank and Worldwide Resume/Talent Bank. Prospective employers can then screen your resume at their convenience.

Another feature often included in career programs on the Internet is a section on resumes. Often, there is useful information on how to write a resume and how to order a professionally written one. More importantly, there are often samples of resumes. On America Online, this is called the "resume template" section. Along with the resume section, you may find information on cover letters as well.

Other information which sometimes can be found online are self-employment databases and Federal employment agencies. This section offers many different documents which you can download to your computer. Other sections offered in AOL include various employment agencies and their locations. In addition, there is often a section for employer contacts. This section will allow you to search for a name or address of a contact in a certain organization or field of interest. Usually, you can search by industry, company name, stock market symbol ticker, city or other pertinent information. You will then receive the address and name of the contact for that particular area.

"Help wanted" ads are yet another feature available online. The Help Wanted USA program on America Online has its own icon for easy access. In this area, you simply type in the field of interest and the database is searched accordingly. For example, you may want to look for a job in marketing. You would type "marketing" in at the prompt and the program will retrieve a list of all the marketing jobs in the current database. The job listings are usually arranged by state or city in order to help organize your choices. After choosing the listing, you can see the job description and the name of the contact person.

For further information, a list of recommended Internet addresses is provided on the following page. These are Internet addresses containing various links to the resources previously mentioned. Most Internet access providers allow for the user to directly type in the appropriate address.

In essence, the Internet provides job seekers with the opportunities to seek employment opportunities while also allowing the employer the availability of a wide range of resumes. Many companies are starting to use the Internet and the "information superhighway" to conduct business. Don't be left behind.

# Recommended Internet Addresses
## for Career Success

**American Job Net**
http://www.galstar.com/%7Eactionst/ajn.htm.html

**America's Job Bank**
http://www.ajb.dni.us/about.html

**Career Magazine**
http://careermag.com/careermag/

**Career Mosaic**
http://www.careermosaic.com/cm/

**Career Shop**
hhtp://www.tenkey.com/CareerShop.htm

**Career Web**
http://www.cweb.com/

**Employment Opportunities and Resume Postings**
http://galaxy.einet.net/GS/employment.html

**E*Span**
http://www.espan.com/

**Government Jobs**
http://205.216.146.66/business_and_economy/
employment/jobs/government

**Help Wanted**
http://www.helpwanted.com/

**Job Connection**
   http://www.jobconnection.com/

**Job Info Center:**
   http://tvp.com/vpjic.html

**Job Information Center**
   http://tvp.com/vpjic.html

**Job Network**
   http://www.conquest-prod.com/resume.html

**The Monster Board**
   http://www.monster.com/home.html

**Nation Job Online**
   http://www.nationjob.com/

**Online Career Center:**
   http://www.occ.com/occ/SearchJobs.html

**Webdog's Job Hunt**
   http://itec.sfsu.edu/jobs/bestjobs.html

# 7

## Dressing the Part

"Dressing the Part" describes the appropriate attire to be worn during an interview. It is important to remember that about 85% of what you convey to others is through non-verbal communication. Therefore, your dress and visual presence can have a profound effect on your chances of obtaining the position. Although this book may not give every possible example of what should be worn for every type of job interview, general suggestions can be adapted to all situations.

One of the most important issues to note in this section is that PERCEPTION is everything! How the company views you, how you view yourself, and how you want others to view you all play a role in the "game" of interviewing. The manner in which you conduct yourself is just as important as what you say, if not more.

Knowledge about the company dictates how you dress for the interview. For instance, a conservative firm such as in the financial industry, insurance, accounting, etc., requires a very professional appearance. However, a relaxed or creative industry such as marketing, advertising, journalism, etc., may be more impressed with a little more individualistic style. Regardless of the situation, flamboyance is not a wise choice! You want to be remembered for what you say, what you have done, and what impression you have created for the interviewer.

The way to gain the knowledge about the company is to look around the office during your informational interview. This technique is discussed in the Informational Interview chapter. Look at how the employees are dressed and the differences in dress between the managers and the other employees. You will want to dress equal to the managers who might be conducting the interview.

"Dressing the Part" will help you look your best during the aggressive job search. Knowing how to dress appropriately is crucial, but be sure to also add your own creativity to your style. You will be given the general details which each gender should follow. This chapter is then broken down into the specific dress codes particular to male and female.

The minute details are the most critical. When these are neglected, you could be jeopardizing your possibility of employment. General hygiene, is the first basic point to cover. Make sure you are fully clean and personally groomed. This means your fingernails must be trimmed and neat, your hair combed, and your clothes neatly pressed. Your personal appearance and cleanliness are vital to the first impression. Remember the first impression is the one that stays in the interviewer's mind the longest.

Make sure you give yourself a thorough examination in the mirror before you leave the house. Check yourself over thoroughly, over-looking nothing. Check for stains in your clothing. Make sure your hair is combed, your teeth are clean, your fingernails clean and that you didn't miss a belt loop. Check that you did not overdo the cologne, that your nylons are free from runs, and that your face and neck are clean. When you look in the mirror, you must feel good about your appearance and no longer need to focus on it. Focus on what you want to say during the interview. Give the interviewer your best for their first impression. Take care of yourself and your appearance.

Now, let's talk about what you should wear. Always dress more conservatively than less conservatively if the interviewing situation is unknown. Never wear anything that identifies any beliefs or personal associations. These items include any clothing associated with a particular area, religious signs or symbols, political buttons, or other paraphenalia. You do not want to distract the interviewer and take their minds off of your qualities and accomplishments. Avoid wearing any items that are considered masculine for a woman and feminine for a male. For example, a woman should not wear a man's neck tie and men should not wear earrings. Also, remember to dress as well as your interviewer and make sure you are comfortable. Your comfort could be your best friend during the interview. You might want to wear your interview clothes around the house or out on an appointment. As you become comfortable in this attire, you will be able to relax more for the interview.

## Women

The most important thing to consider when choosing the clothing for an interview is the fit. Uncomfortable clothing will make an already uncomfortable situation worse. You have more important things to worry about than, for example, a suit being too tight. It is recommended that if you plan to shop for an interview suit, be sure to do it a couple of weeks ahead of time. This will allow you to choose the best fitting clothing without having to scramble for something to wear at the last minute. Shopping early will also give you the opportunity to shop for matching accessories.

The most common recommendation for women's interviewing attire is a suit. A basic blazer and matching skirt will do just fine. Although, we like to think that in today's culture, women can be free from feminine stereotypes, slacks are still considered a "no-no" in the interviewing stage by most interviewers. Slacks may be fine to wear once you have the job, but are considered less professional attire for the interview stage. Pants for a woman in the interview may give the perception of not wanting to "play by the rules" and illustrate an unyielding or stubborn personality. A dress may be worn but is not recommended for the first interview. If a dress is worn, it should be a professional looking dress preferably with a blazer.

When wearing a suit, the blazer should be fairly conservative. Extra wide collars or other trendy designs have no positive impact in an interview. A double breasted suit tends to look more professional whereas the single is more casual, however, either are acceptable. Try to avoid big bright buttons or other distracting items attached to the blazer; these only divert the interviewer's attention. The skirt should be right around knee length, or perhaps one inch above. Also, longer is acceptable if it is below the calf muscle. Shorter than one inch above the knee is **not professional.**

The type of material can make or break the suit. Wool is the preferred material, however it is important to consider the climate. A lighter weight material may be sufficient such as linen, and quality blends. I stress the word **quality**. You should wear clothing that looks as if it is of high quality.

When in doubt, wear navy blue. Although other colors may suffice, navy blue is still considered classic. Again, depending on the perception you want to instill and the type of company you are interviewing with, other colors may be worn. Shades of gray are also considered to be conservative. Certainly, some sort of dark colored suit is preferred for the first interview. Although, the color depends on your figure. If you are a heavier person, stay away from bright colors. The second interview may allow for more freedom in color choice such as dark green, red, or brown. During the second interview, you may also wear a classic dress with a jacket. A small print in the fabric is also acceptable as long as it is not conspicuous. Pastels are generally not good interviewing suit colors.

Your suit should be neat, pressed and free from lint. This displays to the interviewer a pride in appearance. The time you took to prepare for the interview is taken into consideration. If your suit is wrinkled, it looks as if you did not plan ahead for the interview and do not care about getting the job.

Generally, a blouse should be worn underneath the blazer. Absolutely no camisoles! These do not convey the right impression in an interview. The blouse should not be see-through and should not be cut too low in front. The blouse should be crisp and clean. A white blouse does a good job of giving a bright clean look. Cream or ivory is acceptable depending on the colors or patterns in the suit. Finally, the blouse should not be too frilly or have too large of a bow or other designs. These cause distractions.

Proper accessories can help make a fabulous first impression. Your nylons should match the bottom of your skirt; if the bottom of your skirt is black, wear black nylons, if navy, wear navy ones. If it is not possible to match the skirt, wear nude nylons or taupe. If your skirt is a print, try to match the dominant color in the skirt. The idea is to create one solid flow from head to toe with no distractions. If you have a white blouse, black skirt, and white nylons, there is a distraction in the flow. If you have normal to heavy legs, you should avoid light colored nylons. They tend to make legs look heavier. If you have thin legs, you could wear lighter colors. It is still preferred to match the bottom of you skirt.

Shoes are an equally important part of the attire. Many people do not realize that shoes are very noticeable items, especially if they do not conform to the rest of the outfit. Make sure that they look professional and are shined. They should be "sensible shoes" and not too flashy. Try to avoid decorative designs or fancy bows. They should slip on, rather than have some sort of tying or buckling. Proper fit should also be a consideration as you may be wearing them for a long time. Pumps are good interviewing shoes for women. A small to medium 1/2" to 2" heel is suggested for all women regardless of height. Your shoes should also match the bottom of your skirt. This continues the visual flow without distractions. For example, if you wear tan or nude nylons, wear similarly-toned shoes.

A small amount of jewelry may enhance your appearance. However, the idea is to keep it simple. A nice dress watch is certainly acceptable and usually recommended. No plastic, large faced watches. A simple gold, silver or even conservative leather strapped watch is appropriate. Rings are fine to dress up your appearance. Avoid wearing more than two rings; one ring per hand is best. The idea is to keep the focus on you, not your rings during the interview.

Bracelets are acceptable if they are conservative. Avoid plastic, cheap looking bracelets. Also try to avoid bangle bracelets as they may make distractive sounds.

A necklace may be worn if it is not distracting to the interviewer. If in doubt about wearing a necklace, go without.

Earings, on the other hand are suggested. They seem to set off the face in a positive way. However, they should fit certain criteria. Avoid dangling earings. (Its better to wear none than flashy earings.) An acceptable earing should be small to medium in size and should cover the lower 1/4 to 1/3 part of the ear lobe. Wear only one earring per ear.

Small to medium sized pins on a lapel are attractive and professional. However, remember to stay simple.

The best rule of thumb is to avoid distractive jewelry. Do not wear nose-rings or other piercing at all. Remember, we want the interviewer to remember us, not the earrings or bracelets we were wearing!

Make sure you do not wear too much perfume and always examine yourself in the mirror prior to leaving for the interview.

Many of the same items covered in the women's section also applies to men.

## Men

The type of suit one should wear depends on the job. The rule of thumb is that for a conservative company, one should wear a single breasted suit; for a liberal company, one could wear a double-breasted suit. When you are in doubt, it is better to dress more conservatively. You should also consider your body build. Short or stocky interviewees should not wear a doubled breasted suit. This type of suit cut will make you appear heavier than you are.

It is recommended that the suit be 100% wool. High quality blended suits are also acceptable, but it has been my experience that blended suits often do not last as long and do not lay on one's body correctly after repeated clean. The word you should focus on is quality. You should put as much emphasis on your suit as your resume.

The color of the suit should be neutral, usually navy or shades of gray. Stay away from black suits and pin stripe suits. These suits have traditionally been power-suits and are usually worn by executives. You want to dress as well as the interviewer, but not better. You may appear to be a threat or perceived as a corporate 'climber' if you are dressed more flashy than the interviewer. Make sure you research the company's atmosphere in order to give you a better idea of what you should wear. If unknown, stick with a conservative, navy blue, single-breasted wool suit.

Your tie should also be a neutral color. You want to offset the color of the suit but you don't want to take the interviewer's attention away from you. With a navy blue suit, you could wear a blue, or red tie with some type of design. Try to stay away from pastels or flashy loud designs. Usually, the sales person where you purchase your suit and tie will know what you are looking for and will recommend and match accordingly. Use your best judgment and have your friends consult you on what looks good and what does not.

Your shirt is also an important part of the interviewing outfit. Again, it depends on the color of the suit. A white, 100% cotton shirt cleaned and pressed with light starch is always a sure bet. Again, quality cotton/polyester shirts are also good keeping in mind, quality. You want to show the interviewer that you focus on quality in everything you do. I have found that with a single-breasted suit, a pointed collar shirt looks more professional. With a double breasted-suit, I have found that the button down collar is more professional. Again, this is your judgement call. Make sure the shirt fits well and allows room for flexibility.

The best shoes to wear for an interview are wing tips or nice loafers. Try to stay away from penny loafers and boat shoes as these are a more trendy or casual look. Your shoes should not have tassels or buckles. The color of the shoes depends on your suit. The most common colors worn by professionals have been cordovan or black shoes. Along with your shoes, socks are very important. Make sure they match your suit and also are of high quality. Do not wear socks with holes in the toes or heels. What would happen if the interviewer asked you to take your shoes off to walk in his or her office? Another important item is your belt. Match your belt to your shoes. Also, make sure you did not miss any belt loops.  If the interviewer asks you to remove your jacket, your belt will show. For this reason, make sure your belt is in good condition with no signs of wear.

Remember, putting clothes on a person who is not confident and ready to sell themselves is just putting clothes on a scarecrow. Keep a positive mental attitude. You have worked hard to get where you are and owe it to yourself. Stand tall but not stiffly, and show the interviewer how ready and willing you are to help this company succeed. Good luck and look your best! (See the following pages for a final summary of the Do's and Don'ts  of dressing the part.)

## WOMEN

| | DOs | DON'Ts |
|---|---|---|
| Suit: | Navy, Gray, Royal Blue Dark Green, Burgundy | Purple, Red Yellow, Pastels |
| Blouse: | Silk-Like Fabric Feminine Design (subtle) White, Cream Colored Pastels | Camisoles Low Cut |
| Skirt: | 1" above mid knee Below Calf Muscle Conservative Slits | Higher than 1" above High Slits |
| Shoes: | Pumps 1/2" - 2" Heel Match to nylons or bottom of skirt | High Heels (Higher than 2") |
| Accessories: | 1 Earring per ear 2 Rings (Maximum) Lapel Pins | Bangle Bracelets More than 2 Rings Other Piercings |
| Nylons: | Figure Flattering Colors: Dark-Regular to Heavy Legs Light- Very thin legs Tan/Nude - all | Snags or Runs White Bright Colored Tights |

## MEN

| | DOs | DON'Ts |
|---|---|---|
| Suit: | Navy, Shades of Gray 100% Wool, Quality Blends | Brown, Pin Stripe, Black Poor Polyester Blend |
| Shoes: | Wingtips, Professional Loafers | Penny Loafers Tasseled Shoes |
| Shirt: | White, Light Blue Small Stripe Pressed | Larger Stripes Pastels, Dark colors |
| Tie: | Blue, Red, Subtle Print | Crazy Designs, Loud Stripes |
| Accessories: | 1 Ring at most Gold/Silver/ Leather Watch | Earrings Bracelets Plastic Watches Tie Clips or Collar Bars Hanky in Pocket |

# 8

## The Spotlight

"The world has a habit
of making room
for the man
whose words and actions
show that he knows
where he is going."

-Napoleon Hill

"The Spotlight" focuses on you as the star during the interview, and also the company interviewing you. They are also in the spotlight. This is a chance for you to learn about them, as much as it is for them to learn about you. This is the time for you to shine, to show your stuff and to give it your best. There are three basic stages associated with the interview. The first step is the preparation before the interview. The second step is the actual interview and the final step is after the interview. This chapter will briefly discuss techniques that could help you during the interview.

## Before the Interview

The first step is preparing for the interview. First give yourself a test. Ask your self some basic questions regarding your personal and professional life.

1) What are your goals in 5 years?

2) What are your goals in 10 years?

3) What are your strengths/weaknesses?

4) What is your greatest accomplishment? What did you learn?

5) What was your biggest defeat? What did you learn?

6) What did you like best/worst about your major?

7) What is your geographic preference?

8) What is your desired salary?

9) What are your five greatest attributes?

10) What do you value in life?

These are some questions you may be asked in an interview. Even if these questions are not asked, they will help you to further analyze your goals and therefore allow you to answer the interviewer's questions more easily and thoroughly.

Another thing that might help your interview go smoothly is to practice. Talk in the mirror, to a friend, or in the shower. There are many books on interviewing which highlight possible questions the interviewer might ask. These include: What are your greatest strengths? Weakness? Greatest accomplishment? Why do you want to work here? Why should we hire you? These are the types of questions you might hear during the interview.

The next step is researching the company. Make sure you research the company thoroughly before you walk through its door. Know how long the company has been in existence, their growth in the past five years, how many people they employ, what they actually do and most importantly, what you will do for the company. Two of the biggest complaints that interviewers have is that students are unprepared or know little about the company.

Ask yourself where you would fit in the company, and what your impact on this company would be. Why should they hire you? What can you bring to this company? Look at their strengths and match them to yours. Everything you know about the company prior to going to the interview will contribute to your competitive edge. Do you think the other applicants for this position are doing extensive research on their future employer? You need to make yourself stand out. Answer each question the interviewer asks you by relating back to the company. For example, if the interviewer asks,

"Have you ever worked in small teams?" and you know that the company prides itself in small team orientation projects, you can relate your experiences directly to the small group behavior. Remember, the interviewer is looking for someone they like who will fit in well with the ideals and goals of the firm. Do not make things up. People know when you're lying and you will lose your credibility with that interviewer and most likely, the job offer. These executives talk. They are members of boards, clubs and organizations. Don't burn your bridges. Always be honest and that integrity will remain with you. So, the first huge step is to give yourself the competitive advantage and learn as much about a company as you can. Everything you learn about a company can be used. Even if you don't get the job with firm A, you may find you have an interview with or even become employed by that firm's competitor at company B. You already know the weaknesses, strengths, and products of company A from your research. You are now in a position to intelligently discuss the industry and the two particular competitors.

Once the research is complete and you feel confident, the next step is the interview itself.

## The Interview

The most important thing to remember about an interview is the fact that you are about to make a friend. The interviewer is looking for the perfect person for the firm; you are looking for a job. They have pressure on them to perform for their firm, just as you are under pressure to preform for yourself. You have a lot in common with this new friend. This person is in a field which you enjoy. This person was in the same shoes as you at one time. They researched, interviewed and were nervous. Go into the interview with the idea that no matter what happens, at least you will know a little more about interviewing, and that you will walk out with a friendship. Knowing someone in an organization can be used to network yourself.

Remember, interviewing is a two way street. You may find that you do not want to work for this company. The interviewer is trying to find out what they are getting. Who is this person? Why is this person here? Can this person do the job? Will this person stay with the firm? Will this person fit in with the corporate culture already in place? In addition, you are testing yourself and learning if this job is what you are looking for. Will I be challenged? Will I learn? Do I fit into the company? Does the company fit me? These types of questions are the basic reason you are interviewing.

This is the time to show your stuff, to shine in the spotlight and to possibly gain a new friend. You will walk away a better, more knowledgeable person, no matter what the outcome.

An interview is just two people talking about each other. We all like to talk about ourselves. You have earned the right to shine and to show what you are made of. Welcome the opportunity to challenge yourself and to stand above your competition to get the job!

Be sure to arrive on time for your interview. Try to arrive about ten minutes early if you can. This shows that you are a responsible and dependable person.

It is a good idea to catch up on the latest news if you have not done so already. Pick up the morning paper or watch the evening news the night before. This may provide a topic to break the ice in the interview and illustrate that you are up on current events. In addition, you may want to think of some items of discussion to break the ice yourself. For instance, you may notice the firm's new advertising campaign on TV and comment on it. Try to stay away from political or emotionally charged issues.

You should also prepare about ten questions to ask the interviewer. These questions could be about his or her position, the company's growth potential or how this open position effects the long term strategy of the company. Have these questions typed along with your references. You may want to ask the interviewer if they would mind if you took notes during the interview. Sometimes you may want to write a few ideas, questions or answers down during the interview.

Greet the interviewer with a firm handshake (men and women). This gives a strong confident first impression to the interviewer. During the interview, demonstrate good posture and sit up straight. This shows confidence and pride. Also, be sure to always look the interviewer in the eyes. This shows your eagerness to learn and your listening skills.

You are most likely going to be asked questions about yourself. However, they will often be in-depth questions which illustrate how you handle various types of situations. In fact, you are likely to be asked when you have demonstrated some specific ability. This is when your experiences in organizations or internships etc. can help you the most. Use what you have learned both in the classroom and out of the classroom to sell yourself. Make sure you think about each question before you answer it. You do not want to be too aggressive and seem overbearing. There is no time limit, so take your time, listen and answer the questions thoroughly.

You are likely to get some tough questions during the interview. Commonly, interviewees are asked to give their greatest strengths and weaknesses. Employers may look for all different answers here, but are often curious as to how you view yourself, and what you are doing to work on problems. Focus on strengths that are useful in the workplace such as being a team-player, goal-oriented, or a problem-solver. Be ready to back up these strengths with examples of situations when you demonstrated these abilities. The weaknesses are a bit more difficult. You must stay away from weaknesses that will have anything to do with the prospective job such as being stubborn, fear of speaking, or communicating your feelings. Focus on correctable weaknesses such as saying, "I'm not as organized as I would like to be so I have recently purchased a daily planner." This shows that you know your weakness, that it is fixable, and you are working to correct it. Another such weakness, might be that you have gotten caught up in too many different activities. You can correct this by prioritizing and delegating authority to others. Whatever your weakness, be sure to have some way of correcting it, and inform the interviewer that you are doing just that.

You will probably be asked to give specific examples of how you have handled various situations. To prepare for this, you may want to sit down a week before the interview and think about some situations in which you did the following; accomplished a goal, faced a conflict, failed and learned from it, made a tough choice, and be prepared to share a leadership role you have had. These may be some situations you are asked to describe. They may even help remind you of other instances which could answer some other questions you may be asked.

Under no circumstances should you discuss possible salary figures. An interviewer may ask you "What type of salary are you looking for?" It is best to answer this question with the brief statement, "I am considering many opportunities with many firms. What is the salary range that accompanies this position?" Salary negotiations are not dealt with until you have an actual job offer, which usually does not come until after several interviews. Once the job has been offered, it is best to ask for a few days to decide. Do not jump at it. In those few days, you can evaluate the job offer, responsibilities, corporate culture, and opportunities for growth.

After you have answered the interviewers' questions, you will then have the opportunity to ask some of your own. Try to use questions that relate to the research you uncovered. Use the questions you wrote prior to the interview, or ask ones that you have thought of since the interview started. Although you have written your questions on paper, it is best to have them committed to memory. Here are some examples of good interview questions:

1) Through my research, I have found that ABC corporation has grown 23% in the last year. What steps is the firm taking to insure this continued growth(i.e. new products, mergers, strategic alliances).

2) What type of training programs are available to new employees?

3) What is the evaluation/measurement process for this position?

4) What type of person are you looking for?

5) What are some of the goals of the firm for the next five years?

While doing the research for this book, I interviewed many professionals in the business world and one interview really stood out. This interview was with Steven Marks, CEO of Main Street Muffins. He said, "Students do not ask enough questions. They sometimes think that since they have a degree that they should automatically be hired. I look for individuals that ask a lot of questions and have a desire to learn. You must distinguish yourself. A degree is good, but everybody has one."

The final step is to review what you have learned. Take this knowledge and apply it to your decisions. Later, you can list all the pros and cons that were revealed in the interview. You can evaluate the material, and act accordingly.

## After the Interview

No matter what happens, send a hand written thank-you letter or note to the interviewer and to the administrator who scheduled you. This is usually done 24 to 48 hours after the interview.

After the interview, you may receive a call for a second interview. Pay careful attention to your answering machine. If you were an employer calling a student for a job interview, and you heard the typical "Hey dude! Bill and Tim aren't here. Leave a message after the tone," you would think the student was just like every stereotypical college student. One thing you could do is to get one of your friends to leave the greeting. If you live with a bunch of guys, then get a girl to leave the greeting. If you live with girls, let a guy leave the greeting. This will tend to convey a more professional atmosphere. The greeting could sound like this, "You have reached Timothy Augustine's and Bill Chan's answering service, please leave a detailed message and your call will be promptly returned."

Believe me, if I were an employer I would think that this student hires an answering service and really focuses on detail. Now, who would leave a better impression, the typical student or the student who pays attention to detail? This is just a small example of detail. The fact that you print out each one of your resumes rather than mass copying them to mail is detail. The fact that you hand-write your thank-you cards is another detail. Everything you do must be detail-oriented to distinguish yourself from the other thousands of college students looking for a job.

# 9

## After the Interview

"Choose a job
you love,
and
you will never
have to work
a day
in your life."

-Confucius

Okay, you've had your first interview and followed up with a thank you note. Your next step may be waiting a while. During this stage of the game, the key word is patience. Don't rush into anything and lose your chances or present yourself as being desperate. Often, the interviewer will tell you during the interview, the time frame for making a decision or what the hiring process entails. This may include giving you a call in a week or sending you literature in the mail. The interviewer may set up the next interview right then. Your job will be to find out as many details as you can about the process. If the interviewer tells you that they will call you in a week or so, try to ask the interviewer to specify a certain day. Also, ask the interviewer if you could contact them if they have not gotten back to you. If, however, you do not have any response in the amount of time specified (or about two weeks if no time is specified), contact that interviewer. The quickest way is by telephone, so try to get a business card during the interview so that you may follow up easier.

## More Interviews

Most companies will interview new employees more than once. So, expect to go through between two to five interviews. In addition, some companies may even require aptitude tests or other examinations. Often, at least one of these interviews will be an on-site visit at the company. In the on-site interview, anyone you encounter could be the one making the decision about you. So, be sure to shake hands and introduce yourself when appropriate.

Another technique that is becoming more popular, is the phone interview. They seem to be somewhat informal, but are used to gather more information and allow traveling managers or those out of the area, to talk with the prospective employee. In this scenario, hopefully you will be given a specific time in which the interviewer will call. This will give you a chance to prepare. The topics could be relatively similar to those discussed in a regular interview. Therefore, it is a good idea to think of some answers to various questions and some questions of your own to ask. (*see The Spotlight*)

Thank-you notes should be sent to everyone with whom you have spoken. Make sure you get the name of the interviewer and the correct spelling and address. Sending a thank-you note reminds the interviewer of you. It is always smart to keep your name in front the interviewer as often as possible.

## Rejection

Rejection is a part of life, and something we all face at one time or another. If you are not selected for a position, you will most likely receive a letter to this effect. They will often say that there was a "more qualified" candidate. However, it is not necessarily the most qualified person who gets the job, it is the person who knows how to market themselves. It is the person who knows what needs to be done to be successful. Make sure this person is you! Learn from your mistakes and use this experience to gain this knowledge. Henry Ford once said: "failure is the opportunity to begin again more intelligently." Another good quote to remember:

> "Those who know....know"
> "Those who don't....won't"
> "Those who do....matter"
> Craig James
> Business Unit Leader
> Unitech Systems Inc.

What to do? First of all, don't be discouraged. You may not have enjoyed working for that company anyway. Secondly, send a second follow up letter thanking the interviewer and the company for the opportunity to meet and interview with them. This will keep your name on their minds. Thirdly, be sure to continue to follow up with other companies to whom you have sent your resume or have pending interviews. In other words, don't "burn your bridges" with other companies because you have set your mind on this company. Keep your opportunities open. Finally, do not be afraid to interview with this company later. Often, you may not have met some qualifications such as graduation from college or practical experience. Once you have graduated or completed an internship or other work experience, start the process again if you would still like to work for the company. Your competition for the position may be different and those making the decision to hire may be different as well.

Although this might be difficult, try to contact the interviewer who interviewed you and ask for advice on what you could do to improve. Remember, take constructive criticism and use it to your benefit. The interviewer may give you some beneficial points before you interview again. You can contact the person by phone or by sending them a letter. Either way, follow up with some of the interviewers whom you think may give you some feedback. Do not do this for every interview because you may get overwhelmed. This could lead to frustration and cause you to end the search process.

Example questions might be:

"Could you please provide me with some areas in which you think I need improvement ?"

"Could you please provide me with constructive
criticism to help me with the interview process?"

"Could you give me some pointers on interviewing and on things which I could improve?"

We all need to learn from our mistakes and this is a
perfect arena to learn about the business world from
the ground floor.

## Acceptance

If this is the company with which you wish to be
employed, you will then turn to the acceptance phase.
The acceptance stage of the interviewing process is a
process in itself. After all of the interviews are completed and you are the person they decide to choose,
they will present you with an offer. This offer includes
salary, benefits, vacation time, etc. This is the time
you will discuss salary. You should never discuss the
subject of salary until they have placed an offer on the
table. If the interviewer brings up the subject of salary at any time during the interview process, explain
that you are researching many companies and at this
point it is to soon to discuss any type of salary issues.

There are three key salary issues that you must
consider once an offer is made. The first issue is based
on the job you are considering. What is the average
salary of that type of position? You can find this information in the library or career center at your school.
There have been many surveys conducted relating to
this subject which are categorized by industry and job
title. The second issue you should consider is your
budget. In figure C-2 you will find a budget worksheet
that can help you project expenses. This worksheet
covers every monthly expense you should have. If there

is a monthly expense that is not covered, add a section. This step is very important. Not only will this worksheet help you during the job search process, but also after you get your first job. Believe me, once you have a consistent money supply, it is very hard to save and maintain a working budget. You may want to consult a financial planner as soon as you get that first job. It would also be wise to set up a retirement plan and savings plan.

**Figure C- 2**

# Budget Work Sheet

### Fixed Expenses:
Home mortgage/Rent          $_____
Trash                       $_____
Auto Insurance              $_____
Life Insurance              $_____
Homeowners Insurance        $_____
Health Insurance            $_____
Newspapers                  $_____
Magazines                   $_____
Bank Loans                  $_____
Credit Cards                $_____
Other                       $_____

### Variable Expenses:
Food                        $_____
Gas                         $_____
Heat                        $_____
Electricity                 $_____
Phone                       $_____
Water                       $_____

| | |
|---|---|
| Laundry | $_____ |
| Clothing | $_____ |
| Car Gas | $_____ |
| Repairs | $_____ |
| Other | $_____ |

**Your Expenses:**

| | |
|---|---|
| Vacation | $_____ |
| Entertainment | $_____ |
| Education | $_____ |
| Contributions | $_____ |
| Clothing | $_____ |
| Recreation | $_____ |
| Health /Beauty Care | $_____ |
| Other | $_____ |

| | |
|---|---|
| Total Monthly Expenses | $_____ |

The third issue you should consider is negotiation. Negotiating a salary for an entry level position may be very difficult or even impossible. But, you must consider the offer. If you feel that the salary is negotiable, go for it. The employer will probably be trying to offer you as little money as possible. However, the employer may also have a set salary for an entry level position. You will probably need to make a judgement call. In most cases, the employer will have a starting point and a maximum offer. This range fluctuates with position but can be negotiated. It is therefore important to do your homework and see what the going rate is for that position and even convey to the employer if the offer is below the average salary for that position.

Be careful though. If you are going for an entry level position, there may not be much room to negotiate.

*Never* accept the offer on the spot. Tell the employer to give you a few days to consider your options. This will give you time to consider if the salary is negotiable and if you even want the job.

Once you decide on the offer and you want to accept, write an acceptance letter to the individual and send the letter to all of the interviewers you met. This is what the job search process is all about, accepting a job offer. Remember that your reputation follows you everywhere you go and never burn your bridges. Pay close attention to detail and follow-up with diligence. Best of luck and always give 110%!

An example of an acceptance letter is in figure C- 3.

# Figure C-3

January 3, 1995

John Doe
1011 North Norman St.
Cleveland, Ohio 44118

Greg Jones
Business Manager
XYZ Company
1111 White Road
Cleveland, Ohio 44118

Dear Greg,

This is to accept the position of Sales Associate with XYZ Company.

I am most excited about this opportunity. The position will be challenging and rewarding. I believe strongly in the corporate philosophy of XYZ Company and find the corporate culture most compatible.

Thank-you for giving me this opportunity. I am confident that I can contribute significantly to the growth and success of XYZ Company.

Sincerely,


John Doe

# 10

## Recommended Reading

I)     **Subject:** *Selling your skills*
Becker, Hal <u>Can I Have Five Minutes Of Your Time.</u>
Oakhill Press, Akron, Ohio 1992.

II)    **Subject:** *Job Hunting Manual*
Bolles, Richard Nelson <u>What Color is Your Parachute.</u>
Ten Speed Press, Berkeley, California 1994.

III)   **Subject:** *Communication and Networking*
Carnegie, Dale <u>How To Win Friends & Influence
People.</u> Simon & Schuster, New York, New York 1982.

IV)    **Subject:** *Guidelines for everyday life*
Covey, Stephen R. <u>The 7 Habits of Highly Effective
People.</u> Simon & Schuster, New York, New York 1989.

V)     **Subject:** *What to do after you get the first job*
Soden, Todd <u>I Went To College For This.</u> Petersons
Guide, California 1994.

VI)    **Subject:** *Networking*
The Wall Street Journal <u>Networking.</u> National Em-
ployment Weekly. John Wiley & Sons, Inc. New York,
New York 1994.

VII)   **Subject:** *Companies to research*
Leverins & Moskowitz, Robt & Milton, <u>100 Best Com-
panies to Work For In America.</u> Doubleday, New York,
New York, 1993.

VIII)  **Subject:** *Finding a job*
Your College or Universities career planning and
placement manuals!

# About the Authors

*Timothy J. Augustine*, Author, Comedian, Professional Speaker/Trainer, Staff Sergeant in the United States Air Force National Guard as well as a successful salesperson graduated from Kent State University in 1994 in Marketing and Communications. Tim attained his CTM (Competent Toastmaster) in Toastmasters International at the age of 23. He is also an active member of the Sales & Marketing Executives of Akron, Ohio. His philosophies and attitudes are derived from the Dale Carnegie Course, Edward W. Deming's Library, and the Landmark Forum. Tim was also a member of Delta Sigma Pi, professional business fraternity. He had the honor of representing Kent State and Delta Sigma Pi at a national business convention in California. Other accomplishments include Collegian of the Year, Presidents Round Table, Student Leadership Development Board, and recipient of the All University Leadership Award in 1994.

Prior to college graduation, Tim used the techniques in this book to obtain 12 job offers from well respected companies, choosing Unitech Systems Inc. a software company based in Chicago, Ill. When Tim is not selling software or making people smile at various comedy clubs he conducts seminars based on How *Hard Are You Knocking?* around the country. His motivational, light-hearted style illustrates creativity and encouragement to young professionals.

*Rana Curcio* received a bachelors degree in finance in 1994 and is currently attending graduate school in pursuit of her MBA. In addition, Rana holds a graduate assistantship position with the Career Services Center at Kent State University where she assists undergraduate and graduate students with internship and full-time employment opportunities. She is also a licensed Ohio Realtor with The Prudential Kathy Reid Realty. Other achievements include: All University Leadership Award, Golden Key Honor Society, and Beta Gamma Sigma. She has also been involved with organizations such as Delta Sigma Pi, Women's Network, and the Graduate Management Association.

# – NOTES –

# – NOTES –

# – NOTES –

# – NOTES –

# BRAINSTORM!

## Got an Idea? Like to see it published?

### Send it in!

Did you do something different that helped you get a job? Or maybe you thought of something you hadn't heard of before. We'd like to know. And if we use your idea in an upcoming edition of *How Hard Are You Knocking?*, your name will appear in the credits of the book and we'll send you an autographed copy to share with your friends!

**Send comments (with your name and address) to:**

Tim Augustine
*How Hard Are You Knocking?*
PO BOX 941
Akron, Ohio 44309-0941

Best of luck!,

Timothy J. Augustine

Ask your local bookseller for these
Oakhill Press titles
or order direct.
1 (800) 322-6657

*Can I Have 5 Minutes of Your Time?*  ISBN 0-9619590-7-X
Dozens of useful ideas to help you be more effective, increase
sales and keep customers. This compact, easy-to-read book by
Hal Becker, Xerox Corporation's highest ranked salesperson,
combines great ideas with funny and useful anecdotes to
entertain *and* boost sales.
$12.95 paperback.

*Keeping Good People*          ISBN 0-9619590-9-6
Reducing employee turnover is a serious, bottom line issue.
Keep your good employees, and keep them happy and
productive with the scores of strategies you'll find in Roger
Herman's best-selling book. Featured by *Business Week* and
Newbridge Executive Book Clubs. Now in it's 6th printing!
$15.00 paperback.

*Overcoming the Overwhelming*     ISBN 0-9619590-4-5
Providing practical inspiration and hope to those who face
adversity, Charles King's book is not another hackneyed look
at positive thinking. Anyone facing serious challenges and
setbacks will benefit from this book!
$9.95 paperback.

*Practice Makes Perfect*       ISBN 1-886939-02-0
What is the difference between making or losing sales? According to
Marvin Montgomery, successful sales consultant and head of
Montgomery & Associates, the key is practicing. If your sales team
practices the techniques in this book just 15 minutes a week *before*
approaching prospective clients, you *will* see results. *Practice Makes
Perfect* covers maintaining rapport, turning objections into sales,
creating a practical and effective practice schedule and a lot more.
12.95 Paperback

More Oakhill Press titles to boost your productivity!

**The Process of Excelling, Enriched Edition**

ISBN 1-886939-04-7

Team leader alert! Roger Herman's landmark book on excellence has been rewritten and redesigned to help managers and team leaders empower their people for maximum effect. The twelve essential elements of successful team leadership are presented with relevant updates for the next millennium along with insights into the dynamic struggle for excellence.
$14.95 paperback

**Speaking Magic** ISBN 0-9619590-8-8

Overcome your fear of speaking with easy-to-master, practical exercises, a step-by-step program for becoming a more effective speaker. Perfect for business professionals who must address *any* type of audience, Carolyn Dickson's book provides techniques for improving vocal skills, creating stage presence and developing your own unique, dynamic style.
$12.95 paperback.

**Turbulence! Challenges and Opportunities in the World of Work** ISBN 1-886939-01-2

Are you prepared for the dramatic changes that are coming in the world of work? That preparation could mean the difference between your future success or failure! Roger Herman's most recent book describes trends in motion right now, the critical factors to watch and what you can expect in the workplace, workforce and workstyles of the next 5-15 years.
$22.95 hardcover.

"When it comes to books, Oakhill Press means Business!"